# A WRETCH LIKE ME

**PALMETTO**
**PUBLISHING**
Charleston, SC
www.PalmettoPublishing.com

Copyright © 2024 by Debra C.

All rights reserved

No portion of this book may be reproduced, stored in a retrieval system, or transmitted in any form by any means—electronic, mechanical, photocopy, recording, or other—except for brief quotations in printed reviews, without prior permission of the author.

Paperback ISBN: 979-8-8229-3920-2

# A WRETCH LIKE ME

## A TRUE TALE OF ADDICTION, AFFLICTION & REDEMPTION

DEBRA C.

I would like to start off with a "GOD" story (I don't believe in coincidences). This is what led me to write this book. My mom tells me during a random conversation one day that I should write a book. Later that SAME day, my mother and I were in a grocery store when we ran into (literally-as she was going very fast with her shopping cart) an old friend of my mom's, Robin, and her husband, a retired Pastor. My mom tells her after a huge hug (now, mind you, they had not seen each other in over 20 years), "do you know why I used to touch you all the time? Because you are so close to God." I then spoke briefly to Robin, after which time she looks at me and says, "you should write a book." That's two times within hours of each other. I knew they were His Words, not theirs. The rest is my story. I hope it helps someone.

Born to an alcoholic who didn't want me, at four weeks old I went home with my new family. I had a brother, Mark, and sister, Dawn, who were my adoptive parents, Howard and Doralines' biological children. The day I got there a photo was taken of my older brother looking down at me with so much love. It was one I would later picture in my mind when I felt that I didn't belong. Many years would go by without suspecting that I did not share this wonderful family's DNA. Still, I never felt like I was the "same" as other kids. I guess you could say that I was something of a "genius", creating my own crossword puzzles at the age of 7. I remember being extremely selfish, but at the same time basing my self-worth on others' opinions of me. I took my first drink of alcohol at the age of 14, shortly after being told of the adoption. How could I possibly feel ANY WORSE?!?? I had to have something very wrong with me that my own MOTHER would just simply give me away! I went into a deep depression which was "magically" alleviated with alcohol. It became my new best friend — one I could always rely on change the way I felt. Now I could fit in! I had friends who were cool! I was cool!

One night when I was supposed to be in a junior high school chorus concert, I never made it because I wanted to go to the beach with my friends and drink. That might sound harmless, but not when your parents are in the audience, wondering what happened to their 14-year-old daughter. That memory is one very bothersome to me. There were many instances when I would come home hungover and sick. I'll never know what my family thought about it because it was never discussed. I was super rebellious, and would simply tell my parents, "No, you're not putting ME on restriction!", then sneak out of the house through my bedroom window. Very soon that turned into sex at 14, losing my virginity to an 18-year-old boy who then completely ignored me. This of course fed my low self-esteem and abandonment issues with many more letdowns to come.

When I finally got my first real boyfriend, Brian, I would constantly push him away, certain he would leave me anyway, which he finally but reluctantly did. And so, on it went…same situation, different guy, just fill in the blank. I was sure to suck the life out of him eventually. I was incredibly needy, and later felt that the book, "Codependent No More" HAD to be written just for me. All disappointments, no matter how unimportant, were magnified for me to the nth degree.

A particularly hurtful incident occurred in junior high school, when one of my close friends grew jealous because I had a sleepover with a different friend. She was mad, so she systematically encouraged ALL my friends to "oust" me as well. To a person, especially a child suffering from an intense fear of rejection, this was crippling to say the least. I remember wanting to take my life be-cause of this, but God had a greater plan for me.

I was a gifted student, did very well in school without having to study. This just gave me more time to get into trouble. I got caught for stealing, which set the trend for my entire young life. I felt "entitled" to any and everything I wanted. The word "no" just wasn't in my vocabulary. And a few hours in a holding cell was not a deterrent for me. My drinking was now every weekend, all weekend, requiring my friends to drive my car so I could ride in the back seat and drink. I chose friends who loved to drink as much as I did, the only problem was that most of them knew when to quit, and I could not stop once I started. I still excelled in the classroom in spite of my growing bad habits, so I generally could escape any judgment or punishment.

I met my future ex-husband, Robert, when I was 16. He was a long-haired junior high school dropout who loved beer and an occasional joint for relaxation purposes. By the time I turned 17 I was dreaming of a big white wedding whether Robert wanted one or not. (By the way did I fail to mention that he was incredibly easy to manipulate — it was what first drew my interest). Of course, I got what I thought I wanted, accepting the small diamond ring after instructing him to propose. Immediately, the honeymoon was over, leaving two people with absolutely NOTHING in common — hours spent in front of the TV without a single word spoken. I tried, as I had always done, to fill that aching hole inside of me. If only I had known that ONLY GOD can fill it. So, I sought out geographical changes as my solution, insisting that we move 5 or 6 times in the short 18 months of our marriage. We both had full-time jobs, mine being a secretary to a local moving company. But already with control issues, Robert would have to hand over HIS paycheck, while I frivolously spent mine. I guess looking back, I know that he was able to love another person, while I could not. I was selfish, arrogant, and materialistic, and was not comfortable in my own skin.

I had lunch one day with my dear father and broke the news that I wanted a divorce. But soon after that, I found out I was pregnant. So much for the doctor's opinion that I would have problems conceiving, when at 18 I had ovarian cysts. I decided to stay in my sham of a marriage, hoping that I would miraculously somehow once again be attracted to my husband.

My first child, Brett Ryan, was born on the second of June 1988. I was merely two years out of high school, and I knew nothing about taking care of this beautiful boy. Healthy, but with colic, I would call my mom crying from frustration, and she would come to get him in the wee hours of the morning. It seems if anything was in the LEAST BIT difficult for me, anything I had to work for, I would simply pass the buck to someone who loved me enough to rescue me. When Brett was just 3 months old, I left Robert and moved in with my parents. My drinking escalated very quickly, seeing as I could be a barfly, having two live -in babysitters at home. My best friend, Laura, who drank as much and as frequently as I did, joined me in the bars several nights a week.

Certainly, along with the drinking habit came one of promiscuity. I had hair down to my waist, and had lost massive amounts of weight while pregnant, unable to keep anything down for the first five and a half months. Hence, every guy I wanted I eventually got, but only until they saw my true colors, which didn't take long.

My first arrest could have been easily avoided. That night's conquest and I were leaving a bar, and I insisted on driving. We did not make it out of the parking lot when I hit another car. The law was called but there was no damage to either vehicle, so the officer was going to leave without giving out any citations. That was until I decide, belligerent and mouthy, to let him know exactly what I thought of law enforcement. I then quickly found myself in the back seat of his squad car. I refused the breathalyzer, but spent the night in jail, crying the entire time. The next day I was released, and my father hired a lawyer. I agreed to a reckless driving, which prevented a DUI on my record. In the future were many times I would drive highly intoxicated; I thank God I never hurt anyone. I was a lousy driver even when sober as a judge, wrecking 9 different cars by the time I was 18. I would just go to daddy and be given a new one.

I got a job as a part-time secretary for a construction company and boy did I get a lot of attention. I was for the first time at the perfect weight, so I flirted with every guy I came across. My divorce wasn't even final when I started dating the owner of an irrigation company named Cole. We went to Atlanta for a concert, and I became pregnant. We had a very short long-distance relationship. He was smart enough to know an unstable person when he dealt with one. And being a true Catholic boy, refused to believe me when I told him about the pregnancy. My codependency kicked into high gear.

I began to basically stalk him. After traveling across 3 states to see him, not caring that I was uninvited and unwanted, I had my first abortion. It was then that I became clinically depressed. I saw a psychiatrist who diagnosed me with bipolar and prescribed medication, advising me not to mix it with alcohol. Well, that was much easier said than done. I never even made the effort. Maybe if I had, I could have made much better decisions. I do know that my responses to every breakup were anything but normal. Today I know that most of my issues stemmed from my lack of bonding at birth.

After deciding to go back to school, I became involved in the first of many toxic relationships. It was with an ex-military man named Jim, who certainly drank more than I did. I could judge him quite nicely, thereby not having to look at myself at all. I would exchange sexual favors for him to write some of my college compositions. So, I guess my thinking was askew from way back. We took trips to Cancun and to Philadelphia, drinking heavily the entire time. Soon Jim became physically abusive. At the time I was still suffering from depression, so my sense of self was lacking. Eventually, Prozac came into the picture, and I felt good enough to make the healthy decision to leave Jim. He did not take it well. Instead, he took revenge by notifying Walmart, where I was working, that I was stealing by letting Robert come through my line without paying.

Thus, I caught my first felony. Now I was on state probation, with no chance of completing it when I couldn't remain sober nor take my medications as prescribed. Probation definitely wasn't for me, mainly because stealing became my new hobby.

I began dating a guy named Russ, a part owner of a new bar called "Hoser's". He also paid me to be a secretary, typing up menus and the like. However, there was not much to do, so I would go to the gym or the beach while on the clock. That ended when

I got caught by the other 2 owners. Russ and I did a lot of drinking together, which brought on a lot of arguments. He became physically abusive. A pattern was forming that I did not wish to see. I did not want him to leave me no matter how toxic we were together. It's like even though I began to dislike HIM, he still had to love ME.

The mood stabilizers made me feel funny, so I would only take my anti-depressants. The mania that they created made me feel like I was losing my sanity. I felt and acted crazy but enjoying the feeling I got from mixing them with alcohol. Being manic was the greatest thing ever! Just not so much for the people around me. I was like a tornado moving haphazardly through other people's lives. The book for the 12-Step Program says it best: there can be a whole other chapter written about the alcoholic who is also mentally unstable.

We ONLY recover IF we have the capacity to be honest. I was ready, at this point, to become honest and give up the control I thought I had over my life AND other people, to God in His infinite wisdom. On the outside I seemed to have it all together, but on the inside I was full of fear. I had zero self-esteem, finding my identity only through whatever man I was with, and these men were far from upstanding. I was suffering but would not cry out for help.

By this time, I had violated my probation with new theft charges, hiding merchandise in my toddler's stroller at the mall. Therefore, I am ordered to wear an ankle monitor and to stay home if not at work. Well, of course I am smart enough to find a way out of this, or so I thought. I told my probation officer to allow me to wear the monitor around my waist, since I wore dresses to my job as a secretary. The belt ended up being loose enough that if I took off my clothes, it could be taken off. Robert was more than happy to oblige. I was free to go to the bars, in my cups once again. I thought I had it made until, now living with Russ, he flies into a jealous rage one night because I was a few minutes late getting home. He then proceeds to throw GPS equipment out the door. Needless to say, I had to find another place to live.

And isn't it funny how we can almost always remember the negative actions of another, just not quite when it comes to our own? Bipolar may not be as nasty as the disease of addiction, but it sure runs a close second. In other words, my mania was not under control, so I'm pretty confident I asked for my share of trouble in these relationships. I know that my mother used to say I had a mouth like a barracuda….and well, I am truly a product of my environment.

Halloween came shortly after the "Russ breakup", and I looked SO GOOD in my genie costume, that I decided to hit the bars to show off. I could leave my GPS monitor at home, so why not, right?

Russ had a plan that included my downfall, and he used one of his employees to help him do it. Yes, I was smiling at the video camera while he was filming me, but not so much when Russ sent the tape to my house arrest officer. Again, my daddy's lawyer got it thrown out as "inadmissible". What??!?? I'll never forget him, Michael Flowers, telling me, "Hurry up and leave the judge's chambers." (Evidently the judge asked to see it after the fact). And to put the cherry on top, so to speak, Mr. Flowers even got my probation terminated. By the way, he was so good he later became a judge. I was free and would later rub it in the faces of all my enemies involved in the endeavor. I seem to have picked two vengeful significant others in a row.

Still, I had many friends who worked for Russ at the bar. The Bible says, and I believe it, that "bad company corrupts good character" (and MY character wasn't so good to start with). This is how crack cocaine was brought into my life. I was drinking at my friend Jada's, a waitress at "Hoser's", home when a black guy I had never seen before, Pierre, came over. Immediately Jada and her boyfriend lower all the shades on every window and tell me that the little white rock was NOT crack, but rather "free base". I really don't think I would have been so willing to try it if they would have told me the truth. I remembered very vividly reading about crack on a page in the middle of the phone book, vowing NEVER to have anything to do with THAT drug anyway. The article stated that it was an intense 3 second high, and I wondered why anyone would waste their money on something like that. Boy, would I find out why the hard way. At the time I've got to say I had it goin' on in the looks and body departments, which was why I kept getting the crack for free from Pierre. I would take him on "plays", otherwise known as sales in my car because I always had a nice one. I would stay high enough not to care about much else going on around me. I never smoked cigarettes, and still to this day don't think I even inhaled correctly. Thank God for small favors, huh? Pierre lived with his mom but had his own entrance to a very large bedroom, where he would hide crack in different places, getting it out to share with me every day and night. Needless to say, I had it pretty easy and therefore was hooked very quickly. Soon, however, Pierre got arrested and I was left to my own devices. I had no way to get the drug without stealing and/or prostituting myself, so I did both. When I could get ahold of Xanax, it was worse. I had big GODZILLA balls then!! They should have put a warning label on the bottle because it MADE you want to steal! I would simply put cartons of Newport cigarettes (the dealers' brand of choice), in my shopping cart and wheel it right out of the store like I had all the sense. I never even had sex with Pierre, I simply used him, knowing how big a crush he had on me. Later, though, I would have to give my body away, to support my growing habit. Sadly, I was raped several times as well, hanging out in the hood with no sense of fear. In fact, from the age of two I NEVER had one. Soon I met who would later become the father of two of my children, named "Darrell". But that I will save for later — I could fill dozens of pages with the trauma I experienced because of his abuse.

Soon after my toxic relationship with Russ came another, with a guy named "Kevin", a real alcoholic and mama's boy. I was now using crack almost every day, getting Kevin hooked as well. One night we got a hotel room, and I took his truck to go get some, and didn't come back until many hours later. We end up having a loud argument in the parking lot of the hotel and, of course, the law was called. The cops came with a little surprise...also in tow was the producer of the show "Blue Lights", with me as the star. Yep, the whole bazaar episode was now on TV, but the most embarrassing part was the closeup shot of the rock of cocaine I tried to hide beside a vending machine. I went to jail for possession that night. Later Russ would display this footage on the big screen TVs at Hoser's over and over and over again.

After being on drugs for about six months, there was an intervention one bright sunny morning after I hadn't slept in days. My dad had been talking to my using buddy, "Al", the owner of an auto repair shop where my car was being worked on. My precious father was, unbeknownst to ME, giving Al money for my crack to prevent me from getting it in other ways. Al drove me to my house, me literally kicking and screaming, and placed the tiny rock of cocaine on our kitchen table, explaining that was what had taken over my life. So, my mother put me in the car and she and my dad drove me to my first treatment center "Twelve Oaks". I was NOT happy. I was 23 with no grownup rights at all apparently. These 28 days, costing my parents over 20 grand in 1993, were actually pretty amazing. I was put on Zoloft for the first time, which, per Dr. Beach at 12 Oaks, would help the cravings for cocaine. I felt great!! Being clean and sober was pretty wonderful, though short-lived. Life still happens.

After completing the program, I was told that my ex-husband was taking me to court for custody of our 4-and-a-half-year-old little boy. You see, I had it all under control. My counselor from the rehab was even going to be there for me in court. But the disease of addiction doesn't just go away because of something as important as this day would be for all involved. I never expected to lose. A few days prior to what would be this beautiful child's last day in our home, I relapsed. I started the downhill slide by drinking with my friend at AJ's, a bar in Destin, FL. I ended it with a trip to the hood to score some crack, drunker than Cooter Brown. It was very late and very dark, and I was very mouthy. Out of nowhere I was punched extremely hard in the face. (I have a scar to prove it.) I called my dad, and someone called an ambulance. And somehow Robert caught wind of it, and the judge took it from there. I remember he was GOING to allow us 2 weeks to give him up to Robert and his new wife, Michelle. That was until I burst out in tears and told everyone including the judge that I wasn't going to do it. He then ordered it for the very next morning.

Later I went with my son, Brett, to Kevin's house, and he proceeds to break up with me on the worst night of my entire life. As I write this part of my story, it to this day pains me more than anything else to picture my father sobbing uncontrollably. He and Brett had formed a very strong bond, and they should never have had to be separated in such a way as this. It took many, many years for me to forgive myself. This was by far the worst and most painful thing I had ever or could ever do to them.

Even though I hadn't spent a whole lot of time with Brett, I still missed him tremendously. So, I would drink myself into oblivion to forget the pain and destruction I had caused all by myself. The shame and guilt would only subside with my bottle of vodka and an endless supply of crack, as long as I was willing and able to go to any lengths to get both of them. Also, my bipolar was uncontrolled and the mania always led to stealing and other risky behavior. Therefore, I ended up in jail several times until Mr. Flowers could no longer continue to rescue me, and I ended up in prison for the first time. I was given a choice when I was offered a plea deal. I could either serve 26 months in the Department of Corrections or attend and graduate from an 18-month inpatient rehabilitation program called "Phoenix House" near Ocala, Florida. After listening to fellow inmates, I chose the former, not knowing just how AWFUL prison life would be. "Just do your time!", they would all say. Then you will be free of all 'paper', which was slang for probation.

As I look back now, I know that God would have helped me stay sober from then on regardless of this critical decision, had I simply asked Him.

So off to prison I went in the 'paddy wagon'; several of us packed in like sardines, on a six-hour drive leaving Okaloosa County Jail after midnight. I thought THAT was horrible? I would soon find how much WORSE things could get. Once confined in prison, you become nothing but a number, a nonentity, with absolutely no rights, or so it seems. Told when to get up, lay down, eat in 7 minutes, or starve, and sometimes needing permission to even use the toilet, it is indescribably horrific. They throw you in the cold shower upon arrival, ordering you to "delouse". Non-stop you travel along an assembly line seeing doctors, nurses, psychiatrists, and the like from the crack of dawn until evening when you are finally allowed to fall onto your very thin, hard, and uncomfortable mattress, praying you are assigned the bottom bunk. Because believe me, there are no options other than to obey or go to lockdown, where you are stripped of the little bit you ARE allowed to have. You are in an 8x10 cell with no books, no canteen, and no phone or visitation privileges.

Even for those of us who decide to follow all the rules, there is still a standard waiting period of several weeks before you can even contact anyone outside of this hellhole. You cannot even call home to cry. Usually within six weeks of arriving at the reception center of Lowell Correctional Institution in Ocala, it is possible for some lucky criminals to be allowed to be sent to better prisons for the duration of their sentences. It being my first trip to DOC, I was one of those fortunates, and went to the prison closest to my home called Gadsden C.I. in Tallahassee. Before I even finished making my bed, a lady who looked just like a boy with boobs, named Mozell, came to proposition me to be her girlfriend. Well, my answer was no UNTIL she moved on to her next "target" then of course I had to win like always. From that day on we were inseparable, and we both were placed in a DOC ran treatment program. So therefore, we were in the same dorm.

Well, that is why God didn't find another FEMALE to keep Eve company — two very emotional creatures should not be a couple. Once Moe advanced to the "Honor Dorm", I wasn't having it. I jumped on her like a coyote to a carcass and scratched up her face. This earned me a stint in "anger management", although we never even broke up.

After 18 months with no more write-ups, I was finally going to be released to a work release center in Jacksonville, FL., where Mozell's family lived. I worked at Shoney's Restaurant and met them there. To make a long story short, upon release from there to go home, I came back to reality and didn't ever take a call from her again. That's just one example of how easily I could turn off my feelings.

But let me back up a little to tell you how overpowering the craving of addiction is. You see, when I was in prison, I had LOTS of pen pals. I had some that only wrote me nice letters and included stamps, I had some that couldn't send money but could come visit, and then I had others that couldn't visit me, but sent me LOTS of money!! Then of course, there was at least one that could do it all. Let's call him "David". He took very good care of me throughout my prison stint, and then even more excellent care of me while I was at the work release center. He would come all the way from his home in Key Largo, FL to Jacksonville just for an afternoon visitation session. And David was VERRRYY generous. He would bring me jewelry — NICE jewelry — even though we weren't supposed to have it. Eight months later, when it was time for me to get released, I decided to stay in Jacksonville overnight to drink with my co-workers, namely a guy I had a crush on. So that's what I did.

Even without any drugs or alcohol in my system for 26 months, I couldn't wait to indulge in my cups, not to mention the weed I ended up smoking. I was indeed quite sick afterwards. David came to get me, thinking this was the start of a loving, LASTING relationship. I had other plans. I was going to let him down easy, maybe spend a few days with him at least, for all the trouble, you know? Except as

SOON as I saw the Welcome sign of my county, my mind immediately went to a hit of crack. It was literally like a tsunami, a tidal wave of intense craving like I had never known before. I wanted it, and I was going to have it, just like most of my life. I simply told David to drop me off in the only place where I knew I could get it easily. He had no choice. I sent him back where he came from without flinching. I cared about no one but Debi.

I went through all the savings from working at Shoney's, a few thousand dollars, in just a few days, then worked on my parents' bank account. After that was exhausted, I went to hang out in the hood for days without bathing or eating or of course sleeping. That's when I came across my future baby's daddy times 2. I had known him before when I first started using. I hadn't seen him in years, and he didn't look like the same person. He had buffed up in prison and was clean (off crack anyway). So, I dumped the guy I was with and got into his car, and the rest is history. He had a live-in girlfriend, but not for long! Within a couple of weeks, she was out, and I was in. A month later I was pregnant with my second son, born on THE September 11th of 2001 — yes, THAT 9/11. He was my special child. And that is also my dad's birthday, and everyone knows I was the apple of his eye. Sadly, after my father, in Hospice, held him on his chest, died that November. I was completely heartbroken. Which led me back to the bottle shortly after.

When Trey was 3 months old I left the house and never came back. I had my mother's car including her car phone, even though I had my own vehicle. It didn't take me long to run out of money and rent out her very nice automobile (along with the phone, of course.) My mother wasn't too happy when the dope dealer kept answering it. Soon Trey's father, (who I will call Darrell), found me and tried to bring me home to my infant son who had extreme separation anxiety. But I couldn't and wouldn't stop drinking and getting high; nothing had changed. My disease had progressed — grown to epic proportions — and I was in a hopeless state of mind and body.

When I finally came back to reality, after a week-long binge of drinking and smoking crack, I find out very quickly that DCF had gotten involved. Darrell's sister had called them and filled them in on my absence. I had left Trey with my mother, after coming in to the DCF office to fail a UA test. They came and picked him up, and I returned to my mother's house, finding no baby boy. This just gave me more ammunition to use and try to erase what I had done...once again I had lost custody of my precious son.

Soon Darrell goes to jail for violating his parole, all because of me! I asked (well DEMANDED) that he ask a random white guy in the hood for some crack for me, because I couldn't find any. The white man was an undercover agent. So, off Darrell goes to do a couple of years in prison. Now I had nowhere to live as well as no custody of Trey because he had gone to long-term relative care with Darrell's parents. My using continued, worse than ever. I basically stayed wherever I could, paying for it in emotionally painful ways. Until I met Dedrick.

I moved in with my drug dealer/sugar daddy and soon Dedrick moved in, too. We just had to pretend we weren't "together", sneaking in each other's rooms at night. I ended up getting arrested for stealing steaks from a grocery store. This was my 3rd petty theft offense, so it was considered a felony. My sugar daddy bonded me out for the misdemeanor, but when I was notified that the bondsman had to re-bond me for the felony and saw him pull into the driveway, I went out the back door, jumped the fence, and lied to a neighbor about the reason for pounding on his door. I was (and still am to this day) TERRIFIED of returning to jail with no way out. I soon got caught and was re-bonded out (just as I had been told but didn't listen), and I decide that surely I am going to prison. So, I convinced Dedrick to go on the run with me. Oh, he had just done 60 days in jail, and I actually SMOKED CRACK IN THE JAIL LOBBY BATHROOM while waiting for him to take him home!! Whhhaaatttt??!?! Yep. Fearless, that's me. No, extremely STUPID I'D say.

So, we drive my getaway convertible to BFE (Delaware) and Dedrick gets a job picking watermelons — lucky US it's WATERMELON SEASON!! LOL. Of course, I definitely did NOT do THAT job. I would hang out with the Jamaican drug dealers at the hotel. It was a blast except there was NEVER enough alcohol and drugs for me.

Very soon Dedrick and I were arrested for shoplifting. Somehow Maryland (where we were caught) missed the fact that I had out-of-state outstanding warrants and they let me go after spending 7 days in their county jail. Dee wasn't so lucky. So now I am all alone, that is until I met my next victim. And he definitely was that — except no one could see the horns on top of my pretty head ahead of time. I partied with this gentleman until his money ran out, then he was so anxious for me to go that he paid for a bus ticket and made SURE I got on it. Back to walking the streets for me, just now in Georgia.

I met a man there who liked me enough to take me in. I could usually talk him out of about $10 or $20 a day, which in no way paid for my insanely expensive habit. At least, however, I had a roof over my head. I was now very obviously pregnant, but that did not deter me from any of my evil ways.

One night I had had enough. I didn't WANT to hurt my baby, you see, I simply could not stop with the monkey on my back. I got down on my knees and prayed that God please save me from myself. In just hours a knock came on the door. A jealous lady friend of this man had turned me in. When she answered it there stood a police officer and I was hauled off to jail to finally pay the piper. God had answered me! (I would say be careful what you pray for, but we usually ask for what we truly desire, and if it is in His will, He will give it to us).

I was extradited back to the Sunshine State, and awaited my fate from a judge who did not care that I was carrying an innocent child. After all, I was FAR from innocent. My mother hired Mr. Flowers and even the church director was on my side. She found me a bed in a rehab where I could keep my baby. God wanted a different outcome, so no one was even able to speak on my behalf that day in the courtroom. Coincidentally, (not really), a high school class was visiting to view the proceedings. The judge was happy to oblige and sentenced me to 14 months in the Department of Corrections.

I tried to force my labor to start while in jail waiting to be transferred to the prison. Then at least I had a chance of my best friend, Robin, getting temporary custody of the baby. That did not happen however, so I was destined for future hardships because of what I had caused by very poor choices. I remember getting to prison, now my second trip, and kicking my paper bag filled with my meager be-longings and being told, "Inmate! Pick that up!" Pregnant or not, I was once again simply a number.

Upon release, I still had a chance to be a mother to this baby, a beautiful little girl I named Alexis Nicole Williams. She was 8 months old when I saw her for the first time since they took her from me after a mere 24 hours of holding her. She was a giggler — the whole time my mother and I visited with her that's all she did!

I decided to be a home wrecker and go to see "Darrell", who had a live-in girlfriend at the time. It didn't take me long to break them up and move myself right in to take her place. All I really signed up for was more abuse; physical, emotional, and mental abuse.

The amount of trauma that I experienced is too much to even measure. Darrell and I had a 24-hour crack store in our home. Not to mention the prostitutes he would monitor and pimp out, and then sell them the drugs. It was like the devil was in every room — you could literally FEEL the evil. I cannot imagine what I was thinking by living there while trying to regain custody of Alexis. Darrell was off the crack but on the powder cocaine, and he would snort it off the palm of his hand. The next thing I know I'm failing a drug test, even though I was clean and sober. Apparently, unbeknownst to me, cocaine can be absorbed through touching AND through semen. I raised hell of course, but to no avail. Then I just gave up and gave HER up to the state. I know now that I wasn't finished using drugs and drinking yet….and she shouldn't have had to pay the price.

Now I have lost THREE children due to the devastating effects of crack and alcohol. I chose the drugs over them, is what I used to think. I beat myself up on a daily basis for many years. But now I know that I am an addict, and I always will be an addict. And until a person hits their "bottom", there really is no hope for them. We have to want to be clean more than we want to use.

I continued to live with Darrell and use and drink all the time. That was my whole world. I was trying to drown the pain and numb my thoughts and feelings. I didn't want to think about how I had messed up my life, but the more I used and drank, the more messed up it became.

Darrell was the most abusive person I had ever known or even saw in movies. I suffered a broken toe, a shattered kneecap, multiple black eyes (he "raccooned" me several times), and he nearly choked me to death on more than a few occasions. He was also very unfaithful to me, bringing me STD's, staph infections, you name it. I'd like to say something about domestic violence because it is so important. Once a man, or a woman for that matter, exhibits cruelty in any form, please believe that it only ESCALATES!! So many women die by the hand of someone whom they love and cannot seem to leave in time. If this is happening to you, PLEASE GET OUT while you still can!

During this time I did return to prison for the third time, and so did Darrell for the fourth time. I also became pregnant for the fifth time, as I had another abortion when pregnant with Darrell's second child. He told me to have one or he would leave me, and I couldn't see not being his "woman" — I had lost my entire identity.

The disease of addiction is not only cunning, baffling, and powerful; it is also progressive, as I have mentioned before. At this point I was drinking at least a fifth of vodka and smoking more than $500 a day in crack. Needless to say, my disease was in the final stages. Death was the only thing I hadn't suffered. I could not stop, pregnant or not. Day after day, now running together being I wouldn't sleep for 4 or 5 days at a time. Sleep deprivation, by the way, will make a person more delusional than from the strongest hallucinogenic drug. Once when I had been up for days, I passed right by a dealer that was at my house and went to the hood for crack. I did not even NOTICE the blue lights behind me. I WOULD HAVE had plenty of time to get rid of the crack had I been anywhere near lucid. Thus, another possession charge to add to the rest.

I was stealing all day every day for the dealers to get my crack and money for my alcohol. I never used one without the other. The alcohol was my first love, and I didn't like the paranoia brought on by the cocaine, so I drank. A LOT. And stole everything I could, sometimes going into the same store 2 or

3 times a day. I had to ride my bike to make sure I could get away if need be.

Eventually Darrell goes back to prison and I am homeless. I went into labor on January 4th of 2007 with my fourth child, a beautiful boy I named Austin Jeremiah. Of course, I was using when the contractions began but I tried to ignore them, telling everyone that I wasn't in labor as if that could somehow make it true. I was taken to the hospital by the girl I was getting high with, but I left, right in the middle of my labor. The cravings for the cocaine were not subsiding with the pains of delivering a child. And so, Austin was born positive as was I. He was taken immediately. Darrell had given me a staph infection, so I was not even able to hold him. I left the hospital early, fearing police involvement. I walked for miles, still sore and weary, back to where I knew I could score.

I went to jail shortly after Austin's birth. It was for a misdemeanor this time (surprisingly), so my stint was going to be just a month. Now the rubber would meet the road so-to-speak. I no longer had the monkey residing on my back and my mind was clear. I always wanted to be a mother and God had blessed me with many chances. Now I would be. I worked a case plan in record time, pleasing the judge immensely. I was given my son Austin when he was 9 months old, and his older brother Trey just two months later when he was six years old. My life and family were complete. I was clean and sober, going to 5 or 6 12-Step meetings a week. I had a sponsor and was working the Steps. Eventually I even sponsored two girls. Life was spectacular. Sobriety was bliss!! I put a restraining order against Darrell. I would not let him or anyone else jeopardize what I had worked so hard to achieve. And I definitely was not ever losing my kids again. I learned to never say never.

Against the very STRONG suggestion of my wise sponsor, also one of my great friends, Robin, I went on a dating website at 3 and a half years sober. Since, as in 12-Step meetings, we say our "pickers" are broken, I unknowingly chose a crack addict. Soon he was asking me for $20 here, $40 there — well, you get the idea. I should have seen the signs, but I wanted to be in love, and I figured I deserved it, right? The next thing I know I am renting out my brand-new Altima and spending all my money on crack and alcohol. Addiction is always waiting for us to do the wrong thing. It rears its ugly head and infests us like a slum infested with crime. I was beaten once again, lost and couldn't find my way out. Thankfully, to my God, my Lord and Savior, I only used for about four weeks, before I let Him return me to sanity. Because mind you, He always will if we simply surrender. I hadn't lost my children, and that was a miracle in itself.

There was one more relapse that ended after six weeks. But in that time my oldest son, now 10, knew something was definitely amiss. My youngest, Austin, was found to be autistic, low functioning, at the age of 3, so he seemed to be oblivious. Of course, I will never know how devastated either of them had been.

About five years went by with little or no real drama and no relapses. Life was wonderful! I moved my kids into a beautiful home in Crestview. I was on reduced rent housing and worked at a local restaurant, Applebee's. But disaster was just around the corner.

To this day I couldn't tell you how it happened. But I CAN tell you how VITALLY IMPORTANT it is to work through a 12-Step Program! It shapes our whole character and demeanor in a positive way and allows us to live in the world with grace. If we do not behave in a kind way to others and we continue to hold resentments, we will again be uncomfortable in our own skin. An addict will only be uncomfortable for so long before he or she reaches out for a solution — immediate gratification. And for us, to drink is to die.

It started because I had a favorite child, Austin, and Trey knew it. I also needed a lot of help with him. Trey was diagnosed with Oppositional Defiant Disorder, or O.D.D. a few years prior. I was too busy back in my addiction and in my selfish ways to stop the abuse Trey was exhibiting towards his little brother. One day he put bruises on Austin. I sent them both to school anyway. I couldn't be bothered with keeping Austin at home until the bruises healed. God had intervened, was really what happened. He will always protect His children. I wasn't being the mother He intended for me to be and there would be lasting negative consequences. DCF was called and they came to my house, as I was packing. I hadn't paid my rent in a couple of months and was being evicted. I was given a mouth swab drug test, but I was crying so hard it wouldn't register. Still, they removed my kids immediately.

This was the second removal so there was nothing anyone could do. And even if there were, now I was too far gone. I remember crying EVERY DAY for at least nine months no matter how much alcohol and crack I had. I went to jail soon after the dealer I had rented my car to totaled it. I was on my way back to prison for the fourth time for stealing again. All that time I had been abstinent didn't matter to my disease nor did it stifle its terrible effects. It, in fact, had progressed just like I knew it would.

Now by this time I had been to at least 17 different rehabilitation centers. Some I would graduate from, some I would leave, and some I would be ASKED to leave.

Upon release from prison, I did attempt to work a program for a short period of time. It was then that

I met my next significant other on Facebook. I will call him "Steve".

I was living in Pensacola and so was he. I so very much wanted to be wanted, and I searched for that in Steve right away. Now this was when Covid 19 allowed for $1,400.00 stimulus checks. When Steve received his, I was at his house, and I got a surprise. He entered the room and blew crack smoke in my face! Well, you can figure out the rest. It was on!! we began to steal as a tag team. We were "off the chain" so to speak. Soon we were caught and put on probation. Neither of us showed up to anything we were supposed to, and warrants were issued for both of us. A dealer we were stealing for turned us in. Steve actually had the Sheriff's department, the Ft. Walton Beach police department AND the Feds looking for him!

My last arrest was on September 30, 2021. God had saved me again! I prayed all day every day for Him NOT to send me to prison for the FIFTH time. He moved for me in an awesome way! I prayed that the voice of the D.A. over my cases would be silenced, and that is exactly what happened at my bond hearing. I had asked, through my public defender, to be released to ANOTHER treatment center. What???!!! There was no chance for that according to EVERYONE .... oh, BUT GOD!! He answered my heartfelt prayers, and I was released to a four month long intense outpatient program.

After graduation, I began talking to my mother again after YEARS of being estranged from my entire family. (Another answered prayer). Hurricane Ian hit the city I was living in, Ft. Myers, on September 30th of 2022. Yes, the exact date one year after my arrest. On October first, I had been invited back home to live with my mother, and that is where I have been ever since. ALL GLORY TO GOD!!! My sobriety date is 10/1/21.

Now I'd like to tell you what it is like today. I don't worry about tomorrow because I KNOW that God's got me. The book for the 12-Step Program tells us that we must not regret the past nor shut the door on it. So, I tell my story, hoping it will help someone suffering like I was. The rewards of a life in a 12-Step Program are too many for me to count, share but I will talk about a few of them.

Because my God is a loving and forgiving God, I am able to be reconciled with my family, namely my mother, who is nearly 90 years old. She needs not the old destructive Debi — a description I always liked was we are like tornados ripping through the lives of others — but the new and improved Debi. God has changed me from the inside out and He did it through the program of A.A. I am able to live a very comfortable life in the same home that I grew up in. I no longer have to live on the streets and in abandoned buildings not knowing when I would next eat a decent meal. I find true happiness in helping my mom instead of only thinking of myself like I did for so many years. To think what she put up with! It's the LEAST I can do to return the favor. When I get frustrated with her I remember that. It wasn't an accident that the other day I was listening to Joyce Meyer, and she was talking about how difficult it was taking care of her father, aunt, and uncle before they died. But she also said it was the most rewarding and closest time with God. We don't always WANT to do things, but that surely doesn't mean we shouldn't do them.

I am also able to drive a car instead of walking or riding a bicycle in the heat of the summer or bitter cold of the winter, looking for my next drink or fix. I am able to be responsible, show up for work and perform tasks with a good attitude when before I complained constantly, IF I went to work at all. I couldn't fathom attempting to make an honest living while my disease was telling me to lie, cheat and steal instead.

Now I have freedom, not just in the physical sense, but emotionally as well. It doesn't come overnight or easily. After all we didn't get in this condition that way, right? Eventually, though, thinking of others as more important than ourselves will be second nature, as long as we work on it one day at a time. I go back through my day and if I was wrong or if I hurt anyone, I immediately make whatever amends are necessary. I do that because it was through our defective relationships with others that led us to our alcoholism in the first place. We didn't know how to be a friend or a daughter or son or parent. So now we learn. After all, the growth of my maturity level ceased when I picked up my first drink.

I have happiness today. I find that it increases immensely when I am NOT concerned with myself but am genuinely interested in helping others. And who wouldn't want to find true happiness? I found it by practicing the principles of this program. All those years I could have sworn that I could find it through a drink or even shopping or sex or even love. Except that the hole I have inside — and I believe each of us have — is one only GOD can fill. All I have to do is let Him, and He carries me through all of life's problems WITHOUT the need or desire to pick up a drink or a drug.

I have a program today, a guideline to solving problems effectively. Not perfectly by any means, but I can now have real peace, God's peace, for the first time in my life. And best of all, I can help others to come out of the darkness because I was there for so long. I can tell you that right now it may look hard or even impossible to stay clean and sober. But I am living proof that ANYTHING is possible. The decision is yours and only yours. It's the best one I ever made! This life is so worth it! All these promises are not just things hoped for that are written in some book. They all come true for every single one of us in this program. It is what I wish for all of you.

www.ingramcontent.com/pod-product-compliance
Lightning Source LLC
LaVergne TN
LVHW092100060526
838201LV00047B/1494